Praise

In this remarkable book, Odders-White and Love make the case for academic leadership from a person's full self. It's not one more of dozens of how-to books on leadership; instead it's a guide to self-understanding—how to use all of one's qualities in different combinations to be effective, to listen, to be open to others, and to be not just a leader but a human person. The book is a clarion call to academic leaders to take a step back and to breathe, for self-care, and for simple honesty. It's a must-read for anyone with a heart who aspires to academic leadership.
— Michael Bernard-Donals, Chaim Perelman Professor of Rhetoric and Culture and Professor of Jewish Studies, former Vice Provost for Faculty and Staff Affairs, University of Wisconsin–Madison

This book will energize academic leaders to pursue their professional calling with grace. It reminds us that to be a standout we must prioritize well-being. Moreover, with inspirational guidance, the book emphasizes that authentic academic leadership begins with doing the inner work.
— Lynn Perry Wooten, President, Simmons University

Well in the Lead is the perfect companion for the reflective academic leader who looks within while working with others. With its concise analysis, probing questions, thoughtful prayers, and beautiful photographs, *Well in the Lead* becomes a go-to volume for multiple readings over an extended period of time. This is not a transactional "how to" guide to academic administration; it's a book that helps individuals focus thought, emotion, and energy on the important, and complicated, functions of leadership.

— George Justice, Provost, University of Tulsa

Well in the Lead is a welcome and treasured resource for leaders seeking a companion to time-and-task-management tools that focus primarily on how and much less on why. By helping us reflect on our gifts, doubts, and well-being, Elizabeth Odders-White and Suzanne Dove invite each of us to find a foundation for leading authentically. In addition to encouraging individual reflection, this is the kind of book that you may be eager to share and discuss with colleagues.

— Chip Hunter, Dean, Carson College of Business, Washington State University

This book rings so true that I found myself wondering whether the authors had a hidden camera in my office. Their observations and questions for reflection offer critically needed guidance and support for academic leaders. Elizabeth and Suzanne remind

us that everything crumbles when we lose touch with ourselves, providing a powerful motivation to prioritize our own wellness alongside the health of our institutions.
— Diane Del Guercio, Senior Associate Dean for Faculty and Research and Gerry and Marilyn Cameron Professor of Finance, Lundquist College of Business, University of Oregon

This book is accessible and fun to read. It offers information, guidance, and support for those who aspire to significant leadership roles in higher education. Drawn from their extensive academic and coaching experience, the authors provide practical tools and strategies for achieving success at work with a balanced life.
— Kathleen Hagerty, Provost and First Chicago Professor of Finance, Northwestern University

Well in the Lead's positive messages shed light on what is often a difficult and solitary path. Written with wisdom, curiosity, and prayerful presence, Odders-White and Dove offer college and university leaders a valuable resource for their journey up the academic highway.
— Pat Romney, Clinical and Organizational Psychologist, Leadership Coach to Academic and Human Services Professionals, Romney Associates, Inc.

Drawing on their own leadership experiences, the authors dispel several widely held myths regarding leadership in higher education and provide compelling reasons for integrating professional and personal well-being to achieve long-term success. They also illuminate ways in which leaders at all levels of the academy can reflect on their own experiences and create leadership pathways imbued with authenticity. Just reading the poems lessened my stress, and I found value in all of the questions for reflection despite nearly 30 years in academic leadership roles.
— Soyeon Shim, Elizabeth Holloway Schar Dean, School of Human Ecology, University of Wisconsin–Madison

The balance the authors call us to find as leaders is critical, especially these days. I appreciate that the book does not provide solutions but rather approaches. The act of guiding successful people to reflect on what it means, how to nurture it, and what is necessary to sustain it is powerful.
— Katherine Lampley, Chief Diversity and Inclusion Officer, Bentley University

This book offers a unique approach, insider knowledge of the reality of academic leadership, and is a quick and easy read. The thing that will stay with me is the prayers. At first unexpected, but ultimately appreciated, they are applicable in such a specific way that it's clear they were written by and for

people who understand the unique environment of the academic institution. I will return again and again to these little nuggets of truth to get me through the bad days and support me through those that are good.
— Ellenmarie McPhillip, Associate Dean
 Undergraduate Academic Services,
 University of Miami School of Education
 and Human Development

Well in the Lead

Well in the Lead
an academic leader's companion

Elizabeth Odders-White
Suzanne Dove

nodramaturg publishing

This publication is intended to offer the reader helpful insights into the universal experiences of academic leaders. Examples in the book are an amalgamation of the authors' personal and professional experiences. *Well in the Lead* is not a substitute for legal advice, career counseling, mental health care, or any other form of expert assistance. Please seek the services of a qualified professional if needed.

Copyright © 2022 by Elizabeth Odders-White and Suzanne Dove

All rights reserved.

Thank you for purchasing an authorized copy of this book. Please share it with others while respecting copyright restrictions. This means not using or reproducing any part of the content without written permission, except in the case of brief quotations, and always providing proper credit. For more information, please contact the authors at WellintheLead.com.

ISBN: 978-1-7353189-2-9

To the brave leaders
who transform higher education
one step at a time

♦ ♦ ♦

In celebration of positive
faculty-staff collaborations

Contents

Preface	xv
A special note to Standouts	1
1. Shine light on the dark side.	5
2. Leadership is scary.	17
3. Who are you (as a leader)?	29
4. You can't do it all.	39
5. Perfectionism is a soul crusher.	49
6. Relationships are critical.	57
7. Your words matter.	73
8. Leadership is not for the faint of heart.	85
9. You need to come up for air.	99
10. Things get easier with experience.	109
Epilogue	115
Notes	117
Photographs	120
Acknowledgments	123
About the authors	124

Preface

This is not a typical leadership book. It doesn't include chapters on how to run meetings, set a vision, or delegate effectively, although we believe it will ultimately help you do all of those things and more. This is a book about nurturing yourself in order to nurture your organization* and its people.

In our collective thirty-five years of working in higher education, we've learned you simply can't lead effectively while ignoring your own needs. Not for long, anyway. Toiling 24/7, answering emails at all hours of the night, and never taking a mental break may work for a short time or make you feel "productive," but things will eventually begin to collapse both within and around you.

At the same time, focusing too heavily on your own well-being and agenda without developing a larger vision and authentic connections with others raises the risk of a revolt. We hope this book will support you as you strike this delicate balance, day by day and moment by moment.

---

* Because we recognize that readers' professional experiences vary widely, we tend to rely on the broad term *organization* throughout the book. Please substitute any more specific word that suits your particular context (institution, school, college, department, unit, etc.).

Well in the Lead

If you're seeking guidance here, you are probably well acquainted with the headwinds facing academic institutions in the United States and around the world. Everywhere we turn—and every time we brace ourselves to open an issue of the *Chronicle of Higher Education*—we face conflicting priorities and impossible balancing acts.

We struggle to manage our institution's fragile financial footing against concerns about college affordability. Colleges accustomed to serving eighteen-to-twenty-two-year-olds face declines in the number of high school graduates while a growing number of adults need more education to stay in the workforce. Long-standing governance systems that favor careful deliberation by tenured faculty collide with demands for inclusion of diverse voices, greater transparency, institutional agility, and more equitable sharing of power. The COVID-19 pandemic added yet another thorny crisis to an already pressure-filled environment, leaving many fighting to maintain even minimal levels of mental and emotional wellness.

Higher education leadership can feel like an assault from all sides. Just as we get one fire under control, we realize another was smoldering and is now about to burst into flames. It can feel as though we're running as fast as we can on a treadmill that keeps speeding up ... with hungry alligators or tigers (or substitute the predator of your nightmares) all around, just waiting to snatch us in their jaws if we slow down or fall off.

Preface

In writing this book, we're not providing answers or even solutions; we're offering approaches to grapple with, live with, and hopefully thrive with in the midst of this leadership reality. Instead of running faster and faster on that treadmill, we're advocating for leaders to get off and go outside for a slow jog.

Higher education leadership is a marathon, with a few high-intensity interval training workouts thrown in. Now, more than ever, change is the water we're all swimming in within both our professional and personal lives. Staying afloat requires us to go slow to go fast. It requires that we, as leaders, cultivate in ourselves the same growth mindset we strive to help our students develop.

Just as there are many on-ramps and detours in an academic leadership career, this book gives the reader multiple entry points to thinking about wellness. In addition to observations on what we consider the most essential elements of healthy academic leadership, we have woven questions for reflection, photos, poems, and prayers throughout the book. Surprised? Sure, poems and prayers may not be an obvious choice. But we find them a powerful and effective way of expressing the many emotions that accompany academic leadership.

We share a core belief that higher education plays an important role in society, and therefore we believe in the critical importance of leaders like you. Our colleges and universities need leaders who value the work of their institutions and who recognize the impact they can have on their organizations, on the communities they serve, and on others around them. Until we lived it, we could never have imagined all that goes on behind the scenes in higher education, and the critical impact that leadership has not only on others but on leaders themselves. Leadership is not something to take lightly; it is not a role for the faint of heart.

In our work as academic leaders, we have learned that personal and organizational wellness are intertwined. You cannot have one without the other. In keeping with the notion that we must put on our own oxygen mask before helping others, this book focuses on your needs as a leader first. As a leader, however, you'll be helping a lot of others with their oxygen masks. So we share experiences and questions we hope will help prompt your thinking about the connections between the personal and the organizational.

This book can be read cover to cover or out of order, whichever feels most helpful. We hope you will keep it close by and refer to it when you need a quick dose of strength, comfort, or inspiration. However you choose to use it, may *Well in the Lead* enhance your life as a leader.

> With immense respect and gratitude for the critical work you're engaged in,
>
> *Elizabeth* & *Suzanne*

A special note to Standouts

If you're reading this book, you are clearly a standout: you've experienced professional success and have stepped up to assume a leadership role, or are giving it serious consideration—a move that requires courage and skill. This special section is written for those leaders who also stand out in other ways because of one or more aspects of their identity. We refer to these individuals as Standouts with a capital S. Perhaps you are the first person of color to lead your department or the only woman currently serving as a dean at your institution. Whatever your particular circumstances, we'd like to share a few thoughts with you up front.

We must begin by acknowledging that we could never understand another's experience, and that goes double for people whose identities we do not share. We are both white, heterosexual, cisgender women, and our awareness of being a Standout comes primarily from operating in heavily male-dominated environments. This is quite different from being the only person of color or the only trans person or the only person in a wheelchair or the many other ways we can feel alone or different simply because of who we are.

We also both happen to be married to men whose backgrounds are underrepresented in university settings and who collectively spent three decades working in academia. So we have close secondhand knowledge of some of the challenges faced by academics from underrepresented groups. And we both felt drawn to deepening our understanding of others' experiences from a young age. Still, we want to be clear that we are speaking from our own perspectives, which can't mirror anyone else's.

Although each of us has unique experiences, there are some things Standouts commonly share. We are often conspicuous. Even when treated with immense respect and kindness, we are viewed, consciously or subconsciously, as the exception rather than the norm. And we internalize that. We follow a narrow line between fitting in and sacrificing our sense of self.

Many of us also expend significant—and at times enormous—energy wondering whether the thing that was just said or done was motivated by our identity. *Did he ask me to serve as notetaker for the meeting because he knows I'm thorough and possess a solid understanding of the topics being discussed or because I'm a woman?* Again and again, we strike a delicate balance between naivete and cynicism, self-doubt and resentment, openheartedness and self-preservation. It is a tricky and sometimes painful dance. And it leaves a lasting mark.

When we rise to a leadership position, the choreography becomes even more complex. Our success as a leader depends on our ability to influence others, which is directly impacted by the way others perceive us. Standouts are intimately familiar with the double bind that constrains underrepresented leaders: conform too much to stereotypes and we risk losing half our audience; conform too little and we risk losing the other half.

So we twirl and dip, glide and leap, seeking to honor our true internal rhythm while moving to the beat of our organization. When we're in flow, it's situational leadership at its best. We skillfully adapt to a wide range of circumstances, carefully attuned to those around us. In contrast, when we perceive ourselves unsupported, undervalued, or pigeonholed, the self-doubt and isolation can border on debilitating. There's nothing quite like feeling both conspicuous and invisible at the same time.

Still, these challenging experiences can lead to immense growth. As a Standout leader, we are forced, perhaps more than others, to wrestle with who we are, and we can gain a deep and powerful sense of ourselves and our values through that process. We will speak of how critical this understanding is to effective and sustainable leadership. Staying grounded in our values also helps us see the latest organizational "tempest in a teapot" for what it is—exaggerated drama that has little or nothing to do with us and need not throw us off course.

Perhaps most important, we have the opportunity to develop empathy and gain a true appreciation for each person's unique talents and perspectives, which helps us guide others to otherwise unachievable heights. The key for many of us is developing that same sense of empathy and appreciation for ourselves. When we can step back and truly acknowledge all that we're accomplishing despite the obstacles, it's a remarkable feeling.

So thank you for being a brave and authentic leader. Thank you for continuing to put forth your best effort even when you feel isolated or afraid, and for also recognizing when you need to step back and rest. Thank you for making time to connect with people who remind you of the amazing gifts you bring to this work. And thank you for caring for yourself as you care for your organization.

1. Shine light on the dark side.

> But beware of the dark side. Anger, fear, aggression—the dark side of the Force are they, easily they flow ... If once you start down the dark path, forever will it dominate your destiny. Consume you, it will.
> —Yoda

Filtered

We find light
in unexpected corners,
tucked behind memory,
obscured by worry,
shimmering through
a silvery sieve.
(Elizabeth Odders-White)

♦♦♦

Stepping into an academic leadership role can be both exhilarating and scary. As hard as it is to be a successful faculty member or program-staff member, at least we gain a certain familiarity with our organization's expectations after a few years. Taking on a leadership position may mean choosing a job where the path to success is almost as idiosyncratic as the path to tenure.

Missteps can feel incredibly public and painful, and it seems a foregone conclusion that we'll need to make unpopular decisions some of our colleagues will never forgive. University leaders often comment on the difficulty of building a robust leadership pipeline. Thinking about what's expected of our academic leaders, the hesitation to join them is understandable.

Personal and professional trepidation mix with our eagerness to make the leap to leadership; external signals may worry or even dissuade us as well. We have probably all heard colleagues refer to someone who assumed an academic leadership role as having "gone over to the dark side." Some of us may have even had these words directed at us, or heard our inner voice saying them as we considered taking on an administrative role.

We have personally witnessed open and regular displays of distrust for deans and other senior administrators among our own colleagues. These behaviors sometimes rose to the level of alleging a conspiracy, as if academic leaders were out to ruin the school, with making the faculty miserable merely an added bonus. This can naturally lead to both internal and external conflict when we assume leadership roles.

The sense of conflict is often exacerbated by a perceived lack of agency, especially for faculty who spent the first decade of their professional lives focused on earning tenure, treating institutional service as a much lower priority. Tenure brings

Shine light on the dark side

expectations that faculty members will take their turns in administrative roles. As a result, some merely accept these positions out of a sense of responsibility or obligation to their department or unit, believing—perhaps accurately—"there's no one else to do it."

With little or no training, and in some cases limited interest or aptitude, faculty are thrown into the deep end, and we all simply hope they can swim. It would be shocking were it not so common.

For staff, considerable management experience is typically required for promotion to a leadership position. Still, staff leaders often find themselves struggling to earn credibility and maintain their self-confidence in an environment where every single faculty member seems to sit above them in the organizational hierarchy and a key to success is the ability to persuade without direct authority.

So Yoda's wisdom captures a key reason for writing this book. We have seen how academic leadership can become "the dark side," a self-fulfilling prophecy that consumes those who venture into it and causes leaders—who often took on their role with an earnest desire to make a positive difference—to struggle and sometimes even drown. Given the nature of the work, along with the headwinds facing postsecondary education in the US, being a higher education leader means grappling every day with tremendously complex challenges and occasionally having to make decisions when there are no good options. The pace at which leaders must act is out of sync with the pace of the rest of academia, leading to frustration on all sides.

Within this context, it's inevitable that all leaders—who are, after all, only human—will make mistakes, some big or visible or both. And organizations and their members can be harmed when academic leaders collapse.

Leadership roles can also be rewarding. Elizabeth felt more fulfilled in the time she spent in the dean's office than she ever had in her faculty career. And Suzanne was inspired to enter academic leadership from a staff role. One memorable point in her decision-making process was when she heard a university leader, the keynote speaker at a leadership symposium, tell the audience, "When people ask what 'made' me go into administration, I respond, 'Nothing *made* me go into administration. I chose it.'"

Like the keynote speaker at the leadership symposium, both of us have embraced the opportunities academic leadership roles offer to serve our institutions and our colleagues, doing our best to work as forces for positive outcomes. While we know leadership roles aren't for everyone, we are certain there are many higher education professionals who have the potential to become outstanding leaders. Despite that, universities struggle to find people to assume these critical positions, let alone in building a bench of seasoned leaders who develop deep administrative and leadership experience in successively more complex roles.

The success of our academic institutions depends on their ability to cultivate, support, and retain highly effective leaders. We hope the observations, questions, and other content we share here will help current and prospective leaders navigate the organizational challenges endemic to the academic environment.

For reflection

We don't know precisely what attracted you to this book. Maybe you are a longtime leader seeking support or a midcareer faculty or staff member pondering what's next. Perhaps your dean has asked whether you are interested in becoming a department chair, or your provost's office has invited you to apply for a leadership development program.

Whatever your circumstances, we invite you to take a moment to pause and reflect. We know it can feel almost impossible to slow down, and we also know it is critical, especially when we're running a million miles a minute. We've provided a set of questions we hope will make it easier to get started. They cover a variety of topics, so please choose those that feel most relevant and resonant for you.

Where does the "dark side" myth come from? What are the hidden messages underneath? For example, is it meant to suggest that academic leadership is a betrayal of those who devote themselves to being a professor? Or that administrators are academics who just don't have what it takes to become successful researchers? What messages does your organization send about assuming or expanding leadership roles? What are your own beliefs about the "dark side" of leadership?

Well in the Lead

For those considering a specific new leadership role, whether a first foray or advancement to a larger role: What do you need to know about the role in order to make an informed decision? What do you already know? How might you find out more? What would your hopes be for someone who took on this opportunity? What would your biggest fear be for that person?

Which aspects of your current work bring you the most joy? How might you expand those?

What natural strengths and interests do you feel unable to express fully in your current role? How might you increase your opportunities to use them? In what ways could these strengths be applied to support and motivate others?

How would you describe the academic leaders you've worked with? What are the key qualities for successful academic leadership?

How would you characterize your organization's culture and approach to leadership? How does that compare with where you want things to be?

When bright, committed leaders stumble and recover, what factors may have led to their resilience?

Shine light on the dark side

In prayer

Spiritual beliefs are deeply personal. While we have done our best to write prayers that are suitable for a wide range of beliefs and traditions, they are merely a starting point. Please adjust the prayers to suit your own needs. For example, we begin each prayer with "Dear God," but you may wish to substitute one of countless alternatives, such as "Universe," "All Knowing," "Goddess," "Divine Power," or "Life Force."

And if prayers simply aren't your thing, of course you should skip them. It's all about taking what works and leaving the rest behind.

Dear God,

I am being called into the unknown,
into an unfamiliar, disquieting space.
Though I'm filled with excitement and anticipation,
I'm also anxious and uneasy.
How will I navigate this strange new path?
Will I rise to the occasion,
becoming the leader who is needed in this moment?
Or will I stumble and fall,
revealing myself to be an amateur,
a phony,
a fraud?

Please help me find my way.

Shine light on the dark side

Help me balance humility and confidence in my decisions,
recognizing that the roads appearing before me
were laid for a reason.

Help me listen and trust my own knowing,
honoring the voice that says, "Wait"
or "It's time."

Most of all,
please help me remember
that there is no clearly right or wrong choice;
there are merely different paths
that lead to different opportunities
to learn and grow.

With deepest gratitude,
Amen.

Well in the Lead

2. Leadership is scary.

Abrazo

A skilled leader tangos with terror . . .
vibrant, unguarded, as one.
A whirl of fire.
(Elizabeth Odders-White)

◆◆◆

Have you ever encountered a leader who seemed to possess a special ability or power that set them apart from others? Whether they paced the stage while presenting a strategic plan at an all-school meeting or served as a panelist addressing a major initiative at a campus event, they always sounded confident and self-assured without appearing arrogant or condescending.

We sometimes wondered whether these highly skilled leaders were born that way or acquired those qualities along with their professional accomplishments and positional authority. Whatever the explanation, it was tough to imagine them feeling scared, anxious, or uncertain.

As we have advanced along our own professional journeys and worked closely with many higher education executives, we've realized that this initial impression was mistaken. *Leadership is scary.* Everyone feels scared at times, even if they don't let it show. The leaders we partner with, the leaders we coach, the leaders we have become, all share the universal human experience of sometimes feeling worried, anxious, or even petrified about work no matter how confident we appear.

It's not surprising, given what's at stake. These positions feel intellectually and emotionally demanding, and they are! It's a big transition from life as a professor or staff member. Before, we participated in our department's brainstorming sessions and left at the end of the meetings feeling good that we offered some creative suggestions. Now that we're leaders, people look to us to sift through many suggestions from multiple constitu-

Leadership is scary

encies and, from that input, to somehow define and communicate a strategic direction. We are expected to connect with and inspire a wide variety of stakeholders, ranging from faculty, staff, students, and parents to donors and board members.

The decisions we make and implement must move our organization forward while impacting many constituencies who often hold competing interests and are motivated by contradictory incentives. Faculty and staff members' missteps or miscalculations can usually be handled discreetly for those who prefer not to share them. But leaders' mistakes or failures are highly visible and can have negative consequences on many people's lives, including—and especially—students.

As if these issues aren't enough, the decision-making structures within which academic leadership exists are especially challenging. The shared-governance tradition at many US universities means that faculty and staff are deeply invested in university decisions. Divergent views may be celebrated or amplified, which in theory would lead to more inclusive decisions. In reality, however, disagreement among different factions with power or privilege may dominate, delaying resolution and progress while continuing to marginalize some voices.

And of course, all this occurs in an environment whose members are trained to critically analyze the actions and communications of everything around them. Including their leaders. No wonder leadership is scary.

What are some other specific fears of academic leaders?

- Not having a vision
- Lacking the ability to advance or implement their vision
- Failing or falling short of expectations on a key initiative
- Relinquishing control over important details in favor of a big-picture focus
- Looking foolish, ill informed, or non-transparent in front of faculty, staff, students, the board of trustees, or key advisory boards, particularly when asked awkward or pointed questions in public
- Being disliked
- Being forced to implement mandates from above
- Losing the confidence of key stakeholders

"But," you may be thinking, "people do not expect their leaders to reveal their fears. People want their leaders to project invincibility and certainty." And with good reason: a leader who crumbles in public, who loses composure, or who falters in a display of uncertainty may risk creating a perception they are not up to the task at hand.

Still, we've noticed that when leaders invest energies in an outward display of supreme confidence, there is an inward risk that is just as damaging, if not more so. By pretending that our

Leadership is scary

fears don't exist, by trying to stuff them away, we may create an internal tension that eventually causes that facade to crack. Just the act of acknowledging our worries can relieve the pressure.

Who are the one or two close confidants who are always there to talk through these fears? If we get even braver, we can learn to show some vulnerability more broadly to our colleagues. Perhaps we admit a misstep in one of our efforts. Or, we share how a decision we adopted had unintended consequences or missed the mark on what we hoped it would deliver.

This does not weaken us as a leader. Instead, it strengthens our humanity. If we can let go of the need to tightly manage others' impressions, we gain an ability to forge meaningful connections and to take the well-considered risks needed to move our organization forward. The rewards, both for us and for our institution, can be immeasurable.

Viral leadership

My dear fearful one,
Were you not terrified
long before trees began to burn,
before human touch became toxic?
And now?
To be brave?
"Pure folly," you object,
but your time has come.
As hearts lay bare,
you arrive.
You *arise*.
Your courage revealed,
you soothe and comfort,
inspire and hold,
all at safe distance,
with words
infused with shiny bits of soul,
sparkling specks of glitter in the shag,
catching the light
months past the party,
ever present,
if hidden in plain sight,
sticking to everything,
spreading to everyone.
(Elizabeth Odders-White)

For reflection

What do you fear most?

What brings you comfort when you feel afraid?

What helps you manage your fear? Where might you turn for support?

How do you know when you are feeling uncertain? What does it sound or feel like?

How might you reframe one of your fears, such as by expressing it as a curiosity or an opportunity to discover?

How would it feel to simply notice your worry or uncertainty without trying to change it?

How do your supervisors handle mistakes? How do you handle mistakes with your teams?

Leadership is scary

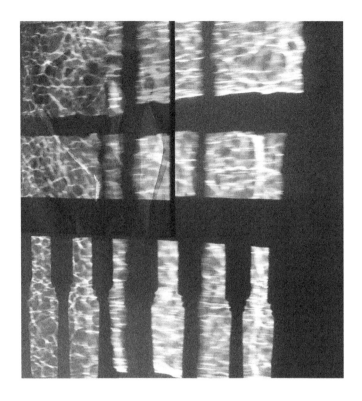

Well in the Lead

In prayer

Dear God,

I am so scared.
Terrified, really.
The problems I'm grappling with
can feel insurmountable.
They're larger and more consequential
than anything I've faced professionally.
And, to be honest, at this moment
I can't imagine how I'll come up with a solution
that honors everyone's needs.

But how can I admit this to anyone?
I don't want to risk looking weak or incompetent.
I have to be the person
who knows what they're doing,
the person who is calm, cool, and collected
at all times,
even if, inside,
I'm losing it.

Of course, even as I say this,
I realize it's a myth.
How could anyone meet the extraordinary set
of expectations I've set for myself?
And why would anyone want to?

Why would we want a leader
who denies their struggles,

Leadership is scary

their worries,
their humanity?

Please give me the courage
to feel my fear without being dominated by it.
Help me remember
that worry is not weakness,
and discomfort often accompanies growth.

Help me seek support when I need it,
and surround me with others
who know and respect the value
of vulnerability and humility.

With thanks for your constant presence,
Amen.

Well in the Lead

3. Who are you (as a leader)?

> The point is not to become a leader. The point is to become yourself, to use yourself completely—all your skills, gifts, and energies—in order to make your vision manifest. You must withhold nothing. You must, in sum, become the person you started out to be.
> —Warren Bennis, *On Becoming a Leader*

Origami spirits

We fold our souls like
paper boxes. Hidden, till
rain soaked, they unfurl.
(Elizabeth Odders-White)

❖❖❖

Who am I? This is the definitive existential question. For some of us—especially those from marginalized communities—our sense of identity permeates everything we do. It drives our vision, shapes our perspective, and impacts our fundamental notion of safety and belonging.

For others, questions of identity may capture less conscious attention. And while a deep exploration of these issues is beyond the scope of this book, the question of who we are as leaders is not only critical but inseparable from our understanding of who we are as people. Importantly, we take on a new professional identity when we assume a formal leadership role, and that identity interacts with all other aspects of who we are. This composite sense of self in turn directs our approach to leadership.

Some of us are built for self-reflection and enjoy pondering the complex questions of our existence, expanding our understanding of ourselves and the purpose of our life. Others experience such scrutiny as an unnecessary interruption to "real work." No matter your preferences, we invite you to spend at least a few moments considering fundamental questions like *Why did you become a leader? What does it mean to be a leader?* and *What will success look like for you as a leader?*

This kind of inquiry is an important first step toward determining who we are—and who we want to be—as leaders. Without clarity of purpose and a solid sense of how we wish to show up, it's easy to become enmeshed in the daily chaos of life as a leader and simply allow ourselves to be blown from one crisis to the next. Setting a vision for ourselves and our careers provides a road map, and our core values serve as guardrails that keep us on our desired path.

All that said, there have been times when each of us has felt completely adrift, with no clear sense of who we were or where we were headed. Perhaps we were running from fire to fire, ignoring our own needs and not carving out time for the deep

Who are you (as a leader)?

and critical work of getting refocused. Or maybe we were so engulfed in self-doubt and worry that we lost sight of the things most important to us.

It is also possible that even though we had a sense of internal clarity, others caused us to question it. This can be particularly true when we don't fit the often-stereotypical image of a leader. The rejection some leaders experience as a result can be immensely painful.

When we lose touch with ourselves, everything crumbles. It's hard enough to be a leader under the best of circumstances. If we don't know where we're going or why, it's doubly hard. And if we've assumed a leadership role purely under duress, with no innate interest or motivation to do so, triple the difficulty. Or quadruple it.

In our experience, there's only one way for anyone to succeed as a leader and stay sane, and that's *their* way. We don't mean to suggest a "my way or the highway" attitude or "letting it all hang out" from day one. But investing in authenticity and being truly comfortable with ourselves is a critical component of well-being, in life and in leadership.

This starts by building self-awareness, taking an honest look at our strengths as well as where we get stuck. Tasha Eurich describes the importance of both internal self-awareness—which encompasses an understanding of our own values, goals, thoughts, feelings, and abilities—and external self-awareness, which captures how accurately we assess *others'* views of the factors above.

As leaders, we benefit not only from a clear sense of ourselves but also from an awareness of how we're being perceived. Only then can we work to strike a balance between authenticity and adaptability. We might ask ourselves, *Do I tend to pay too much attention to what others think, or not enough? Do I struggle to claim my own voice, or do I speak first and loudest, drowning out other voices? Where are my opportunities for significant growth?*

Once we've gained a clear sense of ourselves and how we want to engage as leaders, we have a solid place to stand, even while everything is swirling around us. In a well-known guided meditation,

Who are you (as a leader)?

participants are invited to envision themselves as a mountain, remaining grounded and stable amid the changing weather and seasons. This deep sense of stillness opens up the possibility of vulnerability, a key leadership strength.

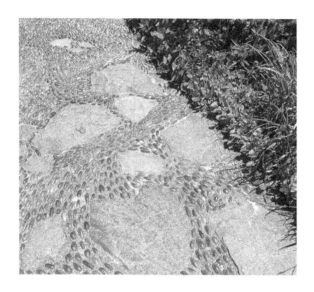

In addition to staying rooted in our own values and purpose, periodically assessing the alignment of our vision and goals with those of the organization can prove helpful. We have found the ability to notice the signs—both those that tell us something is misaligned and those that bring relief and recenter us—to be vital. Our body and mind have ways of letting us know, sometimes very subtly.

Misalignment may show up as physical symptoms, apathy, or irritability. Relief may feel like a sense of buoyancy, a relaxed jaw or shoulders, or a deep feeling of inner calm. It's up to us to listen.

In the end, we view leadership positions as opportunities to learn and grow, to see what we're capable of, and—ideally—to experience fulfillment, joy, and connection. While the stakes can feel high, the decisions we make as leaders are rarely life and death, no matter how impactful the work. While who we are as leaders is important, who we are as people is foundational.

For reflection

What drew you to your leadership role?

How does your approach to leadership reflect the values you want to honor and embody? Are you collaborative, or do you prefer to make decisions on your own? Do you want to lead from the front, alongside, or behind?

How do your preferences compare with the norms and culture of your organization? Are there things you wish to change?

How will you find ways of being effective when you are out of alignment? Where can you find common ground?

What lights you up? When and how do you experience joy?

When do you tend to speak too quickly? When do you hold back?

When do you bring "too much" of yourself to your role? When do you bring too little?

As you continue to grow as a leader, you might find that your identity continues to shift as well. Where have you experienced this? Where might you anticipate further evolution?

Well in the Lead

In prayer

When feeling shaky . . .

Dear God,

Sometimes I feel so clear and grounded,
as if I know exactly what I was put on earth to do.
At other times, nothing seems solid.
It's as if the ground is continually shifting
underneath me.

In these moments of confusion and uncertainty,
please help me access the things I know are true.
Help me see the person I truly am,
the person I was meant to be,
the person I know by heart.

And help me bring that best possible,
most sincere version of myself
to everything I do,
not because it will be perfect—
far from it—
but because the challenges of leadership
require the full expression of everyone's
unique talents and strengths.

Finally, help me bring out
the highest and most authentic versions
of everyone I encounter,

Who are you (as a leader)?

that they too
may grace our work
with their full wisdom and presence.

Amen.

Well in the Lead

When feeling solid . . .

Dear God,

I am filled with a calm steadiness,
a sense of clarity and strength,
a deep-rooted belief
in who I am
and what I'm here to do.
I can feel it flowing within me.

Help me harness this energy
and transform it into thoughtful action.
Help me communicate my
conviction and excitement
in ways that connect with others.

And help me inspire those around me
to discover and utilize
their own unique gifts,
that we may accomplish remarkable things
as we grow together.

Amen.

4. You can't do it all.

Direction?

The Path of Too Much
leads straight to the murky Bog
of Never Enough.
(Elizabeth Odders-White)

❖❖❖

Chances are, if you're an academic leader, you're accustomed to working. A lot. In fact, you may even think that if you're not working every moment of every day, you're slacking. We hope that you'll be free of this unhelpful belief after reading this book, or at least that its grip on you will have loosened.

To be fair, the idea that we should maintain a reasonable work schedule with plenty of downtime, breaks, and vacation goes against the grain for many of us and doesn't naturally align with the academic culture. Academic institutions are filled with overachievers who know how to get things done. Many of us believe in rising to every occasion, which may be part of what drove us to become a leader.

It is a bit ironic, then, that we are often best served by tamping down these urges once we're in a leadership role. There simply aren't enough hours in the day for us to accomplish all we'd hope, and no one—not us, our organization, our colleagues, or our family—will be well served if we're burned out and overwhelmed.

You may have already experienced how easily burnout can become a vicious cycle. When we're physically and emotionally exhausted, we are unable to perform to the best of our abilities, leaving us feeling deflated and pushing us to work even harder in hopes of reaching our immensely high standards (more on this in the next chapter).

This in turn furthers our sense of burnout and overwhelm, and the cycle perpetuates. If we are to remain healthy and effective leaders, we need to recognize and respect our limits. And that means we must prioritize.

Setting priorities is challenging for many, and for some it is nearly impossible. We may be so inspired by our work that we trick ourselves into thinking everything is critical. Or maybe our excitement over each new opportunity leads us to underestimate what's actually involved. Those who appreciate the adrenaline rush of checking things off a list may find prioritizing especially difficult,

You can't do it all

because honoring priorities often entails letting go of tasks that provide a quick sense of accomplishment.

Rather than taking the time to do the hard work of sifting and winnowing, we opt to work longer, harder, and "smarter." We search endlessly for time-management hacks, convinced we can crack the code to überproductivity, thus completing everything on our massive to-do lists.

But it's not a win in the end. Although managing our time and energy wisely is critical, it is no substitute for focusing our efforts on those aspects of the work that are most important and that only we can complete. Trust us. One of us didn't even bother trying to prioritize until she was almost fifty, and the other witnessed the consequences of that approach; so we know both the rewards and challenges of living with intention.

Luckily, we've learned that even baby steps toward establishing clear priorities and living in alignment with our values have significant benefits. For one, we become more aware of the cost of failing to say no, delegate, or postpone when appropriate—namely, that we risk compromising the things that matter most by not aligning our efforts with our goals. And importantly, the thrill of getting everything done pales in comparison to the thrill of spending time doing things that truly matter to us and to our organization, with bigger and better outcomes.

Of course the act of setting priorities must also be approached with care and intention. For example, we may uncover a need to let go of something we truly enjoy. A thoughtful approach that balances the costs and benefits of doing so will likely serve us and our organization better than a more stringent mindset.

Further, even if one could somehow manage to do it all, effectively making every activity top priority, we believe that would be a mistake. First, many of us come into a leadership role with our brain full of possible new initiatives, ways to improve existing processes, and more. Then we're plopped onto a stage in which plenty of the actors are happy with things just as they are, thank you very much. A wise leader takes time to build trust and gain an understanding of the key stakeholders' values and desires before forging ahead.

It's also important to remember that sometimes, stepping in escalates the issue unnecessarily. If we're accustomed to jumping to fix any problem that arises, we may wish to be especially mindful of the chain of command and carefully consider whether our attempts to help may instead usurp others' authority, robbing them of opportunities for professional growth and a sense of shared ownership.

That said, we've seen how holding back can be especially challenging given the headwinds facing higher education institutions, with academic leaders becoming ensnared in perpetual crisis-management mode around a slew of highly visible issues. "How can I even think about prioritizing," you may wonder, "when everything that lands in my inbox is an emergency?"

It's true: much of our time as leaders is devoted to putting out fires. Learning to distinguish fires that will burn out quickly on their own from those that, left unattended, will engulf everything for miles is a profoundly valuable skill that can be gained only through experience. Tying these decisions back to our priorities and giving careful consideration to whether and when to step in builds our leadership capacity.

Along with priorities come boundaries. If we accept that we can't—and shouldn't—do it all, then we must say no occasionally. That doesn't mean it's easy. To the contrary, saying no can be painful, particularly for those of us who like to make everyone else happy. Sometimes we manage to convince ourselves that each yes is no big deal, even when we know otherwise.

The downsides to this approach often manifest as repeated bouts of anxiety, overwhelm, and burnout, until we eventually conclude it's worse to commit to things we can't reasonably accomplish than to set expectations appropriately and give ourselves permission to honor our limits, even if that means disappointing someone. And if we're honest, we recognize that the people-pleasing approach likely leads to more disappointment in the end, so it's wiser to underpromise and overdeliver.

Each of us must decide where those boundaries lie—what we can or cannot do and will or will not tolerate. Where do we draw the line, practically and emotionally? We know decisions have consequences—both positive and negative—that are often difficult to anticipate or even imagine, so we assess and balance the costs and benefits as best we can.

Establishing guidelines or policies can reduce the mental burden and provide self-assurance when faced with tough trade-offs. What are your nonnegotiables? How will you approach common conflicts? How will you handle power dynamics when declining a request?

One of us relies on a "triple-booked policy": If she has two meetings to attend at the same time, she picks one and declines the other. But if she has three meetings scheduled for the same time, she takes it as an indication she's overprogrammed and declines all three meetings, taking time for herself instead.

The other, as an academic staff leader, has developed a set of screening questions to use when facing a power imbalance that may make it difficult to turn down an assignment: Is the suggested timeline fixed? If she starts a new higher-priority task, what existing work can she move to the back burner? Is she the only person who can take this on, or might there be someone else who would find the project a valuable growth opportunity?

While we can't promise any of this will be easy, we can assure you that establishing priorities and honoring boundaries is far more effective than exhausting yourself by saying yes again and again when you know deep down that you simply do not have the energy for one more thing. By focusing your efforts, you'll be rewarded with renewed excitement and a greater sense of purpose. And by being open about your decision to take time for self-care, you become a model for others in your organization and influence the culture. It's a win-win.

For reflection

How can you sense when you are getting pushed too far? What are the warning signs?

How can you shift, making a tiny change that will restore your balance before you hit complete burn-out?

What support do you need? Where can you find it?

How might you continue to build your "no" muscle? What might make saying no easier or more comfortable?

How can you act from a place of empathy and understanding without taking on the stress of others' emotional burdens?

In prayer

When struggling to prioritize . . .

Dear God,

There are so many things I want to do
that I'm struggling to find the time.
And still, whenever another intriguing opportunity
presents itself,
I want to jump at it!
I feel the excitement pumping through my body,
my mind flooding with ideas.

Please help me remember
that no matter how enticed I am
by these shiny objects,
nothing compares to the feeling
of focusing my energy on the things that matter most
and witnessing the incredible transformations
that result.
For that, there is no substitute.

So may I take time each day
to reflect on what's really important,
to align my thoughts and actions
in accordance with those priorities,
and to celebrate and savor every moment.

Amen.

Well in the Lead

When concerned about upsetting others . . .

Dear God,

I find it so hard to say no.
I don't want to make people unhappy.
I don't want to let anyone down.
I want to be helpful and supportive.

Yet I know that sometimes
the most loving thing I can do—
for both myself and others—
is to say no.

Please help me discern a clear response
when I feel conflicted or confused,
and grant me the courage to say no
when that's the right choice.

Most of all,
help me remember that I matter,
that I can't control other people's feelings,
and that I am safe and supported
even if others are upset with me.

Amen.

5. Perfectionism is a soul crusher.

Atlas

When the world turned,
the foundation of perfection
on which they'd built their beings
became the crushing weight
under which they shattered.
(Elizabeth Odders-White)

◆◆◆

The title of this chapter may sound overly dramatic. In our experience, it isn't. In fact, we're not sure there is any way to overstate the detrimental effects of perfectionism. It can grind us to dust if we let it.

We haven't always had this view. At times, we've even been known to embrace our perfectionistic tendencies. Why? Because sometimes it feels as if perfectionism pays off. We successfully achieve our desired outcomes or receive praise from colleagues, fueling these unhealthy patterns. After the fact, it's easy to ignore the frustration, wasted hours, and hypercritical self-talk that accompanied the process, and focus only on how good the achievement feels.

But was the ninety-five minutes we spent rewriting and then rereading and tweaking and performing one final edit of that email really worth the passing "That's the clearest email I've ever read" compliment we received? And why does one of us in particular remember that specific example almost six years later? Grrr . . . perfectionism.

To further complicate matters, when we let perfectionistic tendencies drive us, we have no way of knowing whether this extreme level of effort is required for success. Might we achieve the same outcomes by spending half the time and one-tenth the energy? Perhaps. Maybe we'd do even better. But many of us aren't willing to find out. We'd rather play it safe and feel ultraprepared than risk "lowering our standards."

Thankfully, somewhere along the line we both realized that although perfectionism may masquerade as high standards, it is entirely different. Perfectionism stems directly from fear. It's about protecting ourselves from rejection or humiliation by doing everything we can to seem invincible.

As we climb the leadership ladder and the stakes rise, the potential for intense opposition rises too. This serves to increase our natural desire to armor up. If we've considered every possible objection and anything that could possibly go wrong, then we have nothing to worry about, right? Sadly, we can personally attest that no amount of preparation can guarantee this.

And that's the irony. Rather than protecting us, perfectionism holds us back, reducing our quality of life in innumerable ways. We exhaust ourselves and others with our impossibly high standards, limiting our ability to build strong relationships and delegate effectively. Intentionally or not, we send signals to those around us that nothing is ever good enough. And inside, we experience that sense of lacking.

As a result, we end up working on things well past the point of positive returns, stealing precious time that could be spent on much more important endeavors, like strategic planning—or sleeping. We risk becoming so focused on doing everything to the highest level that we lose sight of the big picture and priorities critical for leadership success.

This all seems clear enough: Perfectionism is suboptimal. It holds us back. So why don't we release these tendencies immediately? For many of us, such patterns are so well established that we aren't even consciously aware of them. They are simply our default approach to managing any fear or uncertainty that arises. As a result, perfectionism can be difficult to let go of under even the best of circumstances.

Now, train us to view everything critically, place us in a high-pressure academic environment, and subject us to heightened scrutiny by others. Soon our expectations of ourselves are in the stratosphere. Perfectionism is pervasive.

So what are we to do?

We could explore baby steps toward reducing our perfectionism, like intentionally stopping when something is short of our standards or shooting for A-minus rather than A-plus-plus work. These are certainly worthwhile exercises, and we have found that even a little letting go of the need for perfection can significantly reduce our suffering.

We could also remind ourselves that perfectionism is entirely inconsistent with creativity, innovation, and growth—all key components of successful leadership, not to mention critical to the health and survival of our academic institutions. And we could try to go easy on ourselves, giving ourselves a break every once in a while and remembering it's okay to be human and fallible.

While we're pleased to have shared these ideas and believe they all have significant merit, they aren't how we want to close this chapter. Instead, we'd like to end by flipping the concept of perfection on its head. What if, rather than striving for some imagined ideal, we appealed to ancient

Perfectionism is a soul crusher

traditions that view everything as perfect just as it is, simply *because* it is? What if we knew that imperfection exists only in our mind, a trick we play on ourselves, a way to create fear of scarcity and "not-enoughness" when neither exists? How would that understanding change things?

For us, the mere thought causes a wave of relief and a sense of trust that things are as they should be, warts and all. And, paradoxically, that gives us the confidence and motivation to achieve more than we could have otherwise.

For reflection

In what ways do perfectionistic tendencies impact your experience as a leader?

How do aspects of your identity influence the grip perfectionism has on you?

What might perfectionism be protecting you from?

How could perfectionism be holding you back?

What if you didn't have to be perfect all the time?

How would it feel to shoot for good enough, or even great, rather than perfect? What would that look like in practical terms?

What if everything truly were perfect, just as it is? How would that change things?

In prayer

Dear God,

I took on this leadership role to make a difference,
and I try so hard to set a good example,
to be patient and supportive,
to truly hear others' perspectives,
to show up fully every day,
and to make wise, thoughtful decisions
that strengthen my organization.

But no matter how hard I try,
it feels as though I'm coming up short,
again
and again
and again.

I don't have enough time
to truly prepare for anything,
so rather than leading
with confidence and composure,
I'm just fumbling through,
running from one crisis to the next
and putting out fire after fire,
as I watch my hopes of making a lasting impact
go up in flames too.

I'm not meeting my standards in anything,
and it leaves me feeling unworthy and ashamed.

Well in the Lead

The voice inside my head
constantly reminds me I'm not good enough,
and I'm crumbling under the weight of it all.
I don't know how much longer I can keep this up.

Please help me see that I don't have to.

Help me see that I'm accomplishing
so much more than I realize.
Help me know that my presence makes a difference
and that even my missteps
serve an important purpose,
by helping me grow as a leader
and showing others it's okay to be human
and make mistakes.

Help me flood myself
with compassion and kindness
when that harsh inner voice kicks in
and tries to drown out all that's good.

Most of all, help me relax into knowing
I am more than enough
and I needn't force or strive for anything,
because I am exactly the person I need to be,
just as I am.

Amen.

6. Relationships are critical.

Composure

"Hello," I said calmly, not breathing,
jaw clenched, like a baby who's teething.
I would often kvetch
over that lousy wretch.
Now I'm smiling but secretly seething.
(Elizabeth Odders-White)

◆◆◆

"It's lonely at the top."
Most of us have heard this expression about leadership. Of course, loneliness may be a familiar feeling long before we take on leadership roles. But in this chapter, we focus in particular on the loneliness academic leaders face, and offer a space for exploration and reflection. As leaders, if we don't address our sense of loneliness, we risk isolating ourselves from our stakeholders, the very stakeholders with whom we need to build relationships in order to succeed. There's a real danger that isolation can lead to ineffectiveness and failure.

To be clear, we're not suggesting that successful leaders must be extroverted and outgoing. Many of us are introverts who tend to turn inward rather than outward and who maintain close relationships with a handful of people rather than a broad circle of contacts.

But loneliness is different from introversion. Loneliness is a feeling that emerges when we're missing the social connections we desire. It can be associated with a belief that we just don't belong, that our background or experiences are not valued. And those in academic leadership positions may be especially susceptible to this sense of isolation.

What drives that loneliness? What blocks a sense of belonging?

If you become a leader within the college or university where you already worked, you may suddenly and disconcertingly find yourself assigned to the "them" camp by those who just last semester were your peers. In the commonly erected us-versus-them divide of faculty and staff versus administration, you have stepped over an invisible line. You may find yourself directly or indirectly overseeing former peers or even former supervisors, and this can lead to tension. You bring past interactions and perceptions—positive and negative—with you.

On the other hand, if you join a new institution in a leadership role, you may find that not only must you confront the loneliness of being the new person but that this is compounded by your position as a leader. When you're hired from outside, you need to quickly assess the landscape and develop relationships strategically.

Some leaders build what they refer to as a "kitchen cabinet," meaning a set of insiders with deep knowledge who will advise them and help them navigate. These are not necessarily the same people as a leadership cabinet; titles are less relevant when building trusting relationships with people who can shed light on the variety of perspectives and experiences that may exist in separate pockets across the institution.

And whether you're a leader promoted from within or an externally hired leader, if there are aspects of your social identity that differ from the majority in your institution, you may be even more likely to feel lonely and face higher hurdles to achieve a sense of belonging.

Although leaders often come across as confident, powerful, and self-assured, we've learned they often feel just as lonely and disconnected as faculty and staff who are not in leadership positions, if not more so. Many academic leaders we've worked with have shared their struggles to develop a sense of belonging in their institutions. In a moment of vulnerability, we once heard a senior leader name the feeling in a large-group meeting: "I just don't know who I can trust."

At its essence, leadership is largely about relationships. And it's hard to overstate the impact our relationships have on our well-being. When they're good, they make everything better. And when they're challenging, they can sap the joy from even the most glorious moments, should a glorious moment happen to occur by chance amid the turmoil of a life overrun with stressful, unsupportive relationships! So it makes sense that skillful leaders spend a lot of time cultivating and maintaining positive and supportive connections to others.

Perhaps we're biased, having spent the bulk of our careers in higher education, but it seems that relationships can be especially complicated in an academic setting. Consider the staff leader seeking a sense of agency and autonomy while worrying about over-stepping within a shared-governance structure that prioritizes faculty perspectives, viewpoints, and input, or emphasizes faculty oversight. Or the associate professor who recently assumed a leadership role and worries about how their decisions will impact their colleagues' willingness to support their case for promotion to full professor. We've both not only known these people; we've been them.

These experiences and others have taught us that relationships are critical and warrant thoughtful attention and intentional investments of time and energy. Mentorship and sponsorship are special kinds of relationship, and for both faculty and staff on leadership tracks, mentors and sponsors play a significant role.

Faculty who enter leadership roles suddenly find their performance measured not by teaching evaluations, research productivity, and citations; these are requirements for scholarly advancement, but they are not the currency of leadership. Staff career-advancement paths in university settings are often obscure, and it can be hard to figure out how to rise into leadership.

From our own experiences and those of people around us, we have noticed that opportunities open and achievements are consolidated when members of the organization's leadership lend their support and endorsement to an aspiring faculty or staff leader. One of the most valuable gifts a mentor can offer is insights about things that lie beneath the surface: how others in the organization experience your actions or words as a leader, how organizational history can help or hinder an idea or initiative, or how you may be inadvertently standing in your own way.

Sponsorship entails advocating for someone who is not at the table. And for people from backgrounds that are underrepresented in academic leadership, having key supporters and confidants is particularly important to success.

One of the biggest leadership lessons we both continue to work on is to get better at leaning into, rather than withdrawing from, challenging relationships. Difficult conversations are difficult for a reason. And as leaders, we have far less flexibility than we might like in picking and choosing with whom we interact. We may be tempted to dodge a meeting with a respected senior colleague who is hostile to a decision we've been asked to implement. We might find ourselves closing our eyes and taking deep breaths as we prepare to take the stage at a department meeting.

But there is a real risk of becoming isolated as a leader: if we cut ourselves off from critical feedback or difficult conversations, we withdraw from our colleagues, which in the end will not help us build a range of positive relationships across a spectrum of stakeholders.

Sometimes the feedback we need to hear may be buried in the crevices of a broader conversation or come to us in a whisper. Because of our positional authority, we might need to proactively open the door for people to voice concerns about our approach or behavior. Taking the time to reflect and stay curious, while being open to sharing some of our reflections or wonderings with a broad set of people rather than just those we work with most closely, is a way of doing this.

The more we practice those challenging conversations and the more we put ourselves out there and speak publicly, the more we find our own edges of growth. Little by little, it does get easier.

Relationships are critical

Academic leaders learn to interact with the vast array of personalities that universities attract. Full of people trained to think critically and seek truth by questioning one another's work, university communities may be especially likely to challenge a leader's decisions or initiatives. Many of these challenges are appropriate and productive, if at times overly vehement. All provide an opportunity to carefully consider how we want to approach our interactions with others, and to reflect on our worldview in the process.

Do we think that everyone is out for themselves or that we're all working toward the collective good? Do we believe in giving people the benefit of the doubt, trusting that their intentions are good unless they show us otherwise, or must others earn our trust slowly, over time? Both approaches remind us of the wise advice Maya Angelou reportedly gave to Oprah Winfrey: "When people show you who they are, believe them."

Whatever our beliefs, they can be acknowledged and honored while recognizing the validity of different perspectives and the objective benefits of being open and risking vulnerability; these are two essential building blocks of a positive culture. At the same time, people who hold positional or social power may use intellectual arguments to try to justify plain old bad behavior—and might even make us question ourselves and our own thinking. This strategy, also known as gaslighting, is an attempt by those with higher status to manipulate through making us doubt our own memories of events or experiences.

In developing a practice of constructive debate that not only allows but invites people to challenge and improve on ideas and then acknowledges those improvements, we model openness to different perspectives. With that solid foundation in place, it becomes a bit easier to counter spurious challenges people may erect for the sake of shutting down change.

"Stars" in any organization, and especially in a culture that prizes faculty autonomy, occasionally get away with terrible behavior. Some people will behave badly in countless ways and never be held accountable. While it may be unwise to give them the benefit of the doubt, we still have to figure out ways to release our anger and righteous indignation or our emotions will consume us. And in some cases, we as leaders have the direct responsibility of holding others accountable for unacceptable behavior.

Calling on our "wise mind," which connects logic and emotion, can help us make good judgments and decisions in a wide range of challenging circumstances. Although this may initially feel counterintuitive to some leaders, the goal is not to eliminate all emotion from our decision-making process in order to focus purely on rational input. Sound decisions result when we seek information from a range of sources—including our emotions—without being overly influenced by any one factor. Thus, our feelings can serve as a powerful source of wisdom when we acknowledge and experience them without allowing ourselves to be carried away.

No wonder we have learned it is vital to invest in a support system that will sustain us during those inevitable times as a leader when we are, or at least feel as though we are, under attack. When we find ourselves wondering whom we can trust, when we experience a sense of isolation at work, it may be a sign that we would benefit from examining our relationships and identifying which are energizing and supportive.

Even having just a few people in our organization who believe in us makes a difference. Finding time to build these relationships is not extraneous; it is essential.

For reflection

What makes a relationship strong? Which relationships energize you?

What kind of social support do you most desire right now?

Who is in your corner? Who will lift you up when you need it most?

Which interactions do you look forward to in your role? Which interactions do you shy away from? What patterns do you notice: Are these a certain type of interaction, such as large-presentation settings or one-on-one meetings, or do they involve a particular group of people? A particular individual? What might you learn from any patterns?

When having a difficult conversation or disagreement with a colleague or group, what tendencies—perhaps withdrawing, overruling, escalating, or other behaviors—do you notice in your own reactions? How can you reframe these reactions in order to continue engaging in ways that move toward a solution while protecting rather than harming relationships? What strategies have worked for you in the past that you might try in these settings? For example, as you prepare to initiate a confrontation, how do you set your intention beforehand?

How might you improve your awareness of any "in group-out group" divisions among your team? How might you begin to break those down?

How do you know when you're entering unhealthy territory in a relationship? Do you begin to frame disagreements as doubts about that person's loyalty? Do you question their professional competence more than you would that of others who perform similarly? How can you get to healthier ground when you notice these kinds of red flags appearing?

If you map your healthy, supportive relationships, what do they tell you? Do you have strong connections in different parts and at different levels of the organization? How might you continue to build relationships across and outside your institution, so you have people who want to step up for you when needed?

Special considerations for those who lead large units: When your role involves leading large numbers of people, you lose the ability to interact with everyone individually and build one-on-one relationships with each person. In what ways can you build and maintain a positive reputation, becoming known in an authentic way while recognizing you can't fully control others' view of you?

Special considerations for staff leaders: When faculty hold much of the ultimate decision-making power, or believe they do, the challenges of shared decision-making impact the tools of influence at staff leaders' disposal. How can you influence without direct authority? When you feel disrespected or not valued by faculty colleagues, even within your area of expertise, what positive messages can you use to reinforce your own sense of self? Where do you experience a lack of agency, and how might you reframe that to focus on what is within your sphere of control?

In prayer

When facing challenging relationships or feeling isolated and alone . . .

Dear God,

How did my relationships become so complicated?

Before I took on this leadership role,
things were pretty simple.
I got along fine with most of my colleagues,
and I even considered a couple of them friends.
Sure, there were a few people
I tried to steer clear of,
but I was rarely forced to interact with them . . .
just the occasional meeting,
when they routinely decided
to spout off about something.

Now my days are dominated by these interactions.
I'm running from meeting to meeting,
and I feel as if I'm constantly
trying to convince someone of something
or trying to justify or defend a decision.

Gone are the days of casual hallway conversation.
Gone are the days of true
collaborative brainstorming.
Gone is the sense that we're all in this together.

Well in the Lead

I honestly sometimes wonder
whether people are out to get me.

Please help me navigate this dark space.
Help me see the good intentions in others
without being blinded by them.
Help me remember that we are all human
and we're all just trying to get our needs met—
some more skillfully than others.
Help me know that, in many cases,
people's reactions have nothing to do with me.
Help me remain open and approachable
while embodying the wisdom
I've gained through experience.
Help me seek out supportive relationships
that energize and rejuvenate me,
and when I find them,
help me treat them as the blessing they are.

Most of all,
help me keep a strong back
and a soft heart,
knowing that you are with me always.

Amen.

Relationships are critical

When feeling grateful for fulfilling professional relationships . . .

Dear God,

Thank you.

Thank you for the remarkable people
in my professional life.

Thank you for the colleague
who through a mere glance,
almost certainly imperceptible to others,
sends me strength and support
just when I need it.

Thank you for the friend
who pops their head into my office
just to check in,
making sure that difficult meeting
wasn't *too* difficult.

Thank you for the many partners
who engage with me
in brainstorming, ideating, and strategizing.
I am energized and humbled
by their creativity and wisdom.

Thank you for surrounding me
with so many people who help me learn,
who broaden my perspective,
and who help me grow as a leader,

Well in the Lead

even when that process is
bumpier than I might choose.

Thank you for all of them.

May they in turn
experience these same blessings in me.

Amen.

7. Your words matter.

They just don't understand?

The meaning of words:
the bridge straddling common ground
and the Great Divide.
(Elizabeth Odders-White)

❖❖❖

Have you ever participated in a meeting that opened something like this? "Okay, we need to work through three budget scenarios—status quo, a 5 percent cut, and a 10 percent cut—and we have to complete the process by Friday. [Insert collective groan here.] I'm sorry. I know it's ridiculous. But the dean is insisting."

If your experience resembles ours, you've witnessed this type of exchange many times, perhaps without even noticing. From one angle, it's a leader empathizing with their team. No big deal, and nothing especially noteworthy. But from another, it's a leader undermining their organization by sending mixed messages.

Let's face it: communication is a tricky business for all of us, leader or not. It's easy to gloss over key points or jump to conclusions without truly listening, both of which can lead to confusion, frustration, and resentment. And when there is a power differential—real or perceived—between the speaker and the listener, words can carry even more weight. Perhaps you've made an offhand comment to someone, only to learn later that they took it as a directive. Or maybe you've left a meeting with what felt like rock-solid agreement on next steps and were surprised when, at the next meeting, the topic was reopened for consideration as if it had never been discussed.

These scenarios illustrate that communication becomes decidedly nuanced when we assume leadership roles. In a sense, our words are no longer our own. Every email we send or comment we make conveys not only our own perspective but that of our organization. Social media has put leaders' communication in the spotlight in new ways, providing both a method for academic leaders and their many stakeholders to connect across hierarchies and geographic distance as well as a place where difficult conversations can become very public.

There's a reason government officials include formulaic disclaimers when making public remarks. Academic leaders might benefit from the same level of discipline, though even that wouldn't guarantee our words are received as intended.

While our goal here is not to offer training in strategic communication—we assume you have access to many other helpful resources on that topic—we do want to explicitly acknowledge the fundamental role communication plays. In many ways, effective leadership and effective communication are synonymous. They go hand in hand. Our words tell people who we are. Skillful, authentic communication builds trust and strengthens organizations, while poor communication can break not only the best initiatives but leaders themselves.

Naturally, this can create a great deal of pressure. We all communicate poorly from time to time, and the emphasis on effective communication may lead to worry that even a slight slip could cause all the dominoes to fall. High-profile cases of forced resignations can give the impression there is no room for communication missteps and little opportunity to learn from our mistakes.

Rather than falling into this paralyzing all-or-nothing thinking, we can adopt some simple ways to improve our communication without obsessing over every word. For example, pausing to set an intention as we walk to a colleague's office or prepare to log in to a virtual meeting can have a huge impact on how we—and, importantly, others—experience the interaction. This could be especially helpful when we're feeling rushed, stressed, or scattered, and before discussions of contentious or emotionally loaded topics.

Sometimes discussions we expected to be straightforward end up going sideways. We've found this to be particularly common in communicating around change. When we ask others to do things differently or to relinquish roles they are attached to, they experience a loss of control. Their sense of professional identity can easily become threatened, especially in environments with high levels of autonomy, like academia.

Simply maintaining an awareness of this possibility and learning to recognize it when we're in the midst of it, rather than getting hooked into the other person's emotions, can go a long way.

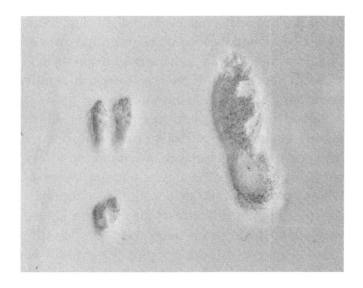

Having compassion for ourselves and our own emotional experience is equally important. It's not only the words we speak to others that matter. The things we say to ourselves may be even more important for our well-being and success as leaders. And yet, troublingly, many of us—often unknowingly and almost certainly unintentionally—use our words as weapons against ourselves rather than harnessing their power to strengthen and inspire us.

We all procrastinate, we all feel overwhelmed at times, and we all have days when things don't go as planned. Why add insult to injury by turning these moments of struggle into proof of our shortcomings, instead of seeing them for the universal human experiences they are?

The tendency to make sense of the world by fabricating stories and labeling them ironclad truths, without stopping to consider the alternatives or the consequences, seems hardwired in many of us. But we can begin to shift that unhelpful habit by simply becoming aware of our thoughts. What stories are we telling ourselves? What limiting beliefs might be driving these stories? And, most important, are these beliefs even accurate? Frequently, the answer is no.

Bringing a gentle curiosity to our thoughts, allowing for the possibility that not everything we think is worth believing, we start to chip away at our negative patterns. Of course, many of these thoughts have been with us for years, so releasing them can take time and concentration. Still, in our experience, even slightly weakening the grip of these unhelpful thoughts can lead to a significant boost in confidence, energy, and motivation.

Interestingly, this kind of inner storytelling also happens regularly in our interactions with others. We glance over at a colleague during a high-stakes meeting and notice a frown on his face. Immediately, our mind gets to work: *He hates this idea. He's going to do everything possible to kill my proposal. Blah, blah, blah.*

And maybe that's all true. Or maybe he's thinking about an infuriating text he just received from his teenage son. The point is, we merely know that we look at him and see the edges of his mouth turned down. Nothing more.

It's an enlightening and worthwhile exercise to try going through the day noticing and describing things that happen without assigning them meaning. When we catch ourselves in interpretations or judgments—*She's so rude!*—we can replace them with observable facts gathered using our senses: *When I was speaking to her, she turned away, grabbed her phone, and started texting.*

But be careful; judgments often masquerade as descriptions. For example, *She demonstrated she isn't interested in what I have to say* may seem factual at first, but it is actually an interpretation; we can't directly observe her level of interest. Afterward, we might notice how observing and describing, rather than creating stories, changes our experience or perspective.

Once we've recognized the power of our words, we can drill down into other aspects of interpersonal communication. As opposed to offering specific guidance, we'll share a few reminders that may be helpful, especially when communication gets challenging.

Presence beats preparation. Sometimes the best form of communication is listening. We don't have to do all the talking or have all the answers. Instead, why not ask questions from a place of sincere curiosity and respect? This may mean spending less time preparing a PowerPoint presentation and, alternatively, devoting the time before a meeting to ensuring we can be fully present for it.

That can be challenging for some, but the rewards are substantial. Doing so helps us to learn what's really happening at all levels of our organization and allows us to demonstrate that we value and care for people and their perspectives. (Our thanks to adrienne maree brown for articulating this principle so clearly in *Emergent Strategy*.)

Pushback is rough. This is academia. Intellectual debate goes with the territory. Still, it can be frustrating and disheartening when people who don't have the full picture push back on our decision. Maybe we shared the rationale, but they've forgotten; it isn't paramount for them as it is for us. Or perhaps the full backstory cannot be disclosed for reasons of confidentiality. Even worse, our colleagues may have simply ignored all prior opportunities to offer constructive input and yet still feel comfortable—compelled, it would seem—to fight us tooth and nail.

These experiences are difficult. Take a deep breath. Try to keep things in perspective. And if we snap, let's cut ourselves some slack (see the next point).

Miscommunication happens. No matter how hard we try, the message will get garbled from time to time. Perhaps one person is distracted or tired, or maybe we simply didn't anticipate how strongly someone would react. Whatever the cause, it's okay to make mistakes, and none of us is perfect.

That doesn't absolve us of responsibility to build an awareness of the impact our specific word choices have on others and to continually work toward inclusive, positive, and respectful communication. To the contrary, giving ourselves and others grace creates the space for real growth. The beautiful thing about communication is that, when used wisely and with thoughtful intention, it can repair rifts or damage, ultimately resulting in stronger bonds and deeper trust.

For reflection

What mindset do you wish to adopt right now? What principles will guide your words and actions in this moment?

What stories are you telling yourself? How do those stories make you feel? What alternative stories might you choose?

How do you want to speak to yourself? What do you want or need to remind yourself?

How do you want to show up for your next meeting? What questions might you ask to gain more insight into your colleagues' perspectives and experiences?

How might you prioritize presence over preparation? Listening over speaking?

In prayer

Dear God,

Please help me find the words
that will allow others to truly hear and understand.

Help me listen with openness and compassion,
seeking the key insights in others' words
and in my own inner dialogue.

Help me pause when I need to
rather than rushing from one thing to the next
with no chance to process
or set clear intentions.

Help me remain present
during even the most challenging encounters.

And when I slip up,
help me remember that mistakes
are part of being human
and miscommunications
can always be remedied.

With gratitude for all of this and so much more,
Amen.

Well in the Lead

8. Leadership is not for the faint of heart.

Haters Haiku

"Why ask *him*? He's staff."
"We all hate the name you picked."
Rejection still stings.
(Suzanne Dove)

❖❖❖

A chief of staff walked into an office. (Yes, it sounds like the beginning of a joke. We only wish that were the case.) "Do you have a minute to talk?" he asked the dean.

"Sure," the dean replied. "What's up?"

"Mind if I close the door?" said the chief of staff, shutting it quickly. "So, remember that new idea you brought up at the faculty planning committee meeting last week? The one about starting a new degree program?"

"Yes, what about it?" asked the dean.

The chief of staff responded, "There's a front-page story in today's campus newspaper—with anonymous quotes from some of our faculty, saying that the dean is diverting funds away from existing students to bring in new students for a new program. Word at the watercooler is the provost is really mad. At you."

Maybe you have been in some version of a conversation like this, either as the dean or as the chief of staff. The details surely varied. But whether or not you've been in a similar situation, you can probably relate to the feelings of these two characters. Surprise. Embarrassment. Fear. Feelings of betrayal. Of disappointment. Of being ambushed by people you trusted.

You may have stepped into an academic leadership position because of your conviction that new programs, modernized processes, alumni-giving opportunities, or better ways of serving students would be wonderful for your university. Some of these ideas may entail major transformations while others might be modest tweaks to an existing program or process. And even a seemingly small adjustment can feel big to someone whose responsibilities are directly impacted.

Academic institutions tend to change slowly. Have you heard the one about how many faculty it takes to change a lightbulb? The punch line goes something like this: "Change? What do you mean, 'change'?"

This doesn't mean universities aren't full of bright people with innovative ideas. Maybe when you were an associate professor in a brainstorming session or a staff member serving on a committee, your ideas were welcomed as "creative" and "exciting." But once you're part of administration, your responsibilities shift. Now your main role is to seed conversations that help your colleagues generate new ideas and then to shepherd them to execution.

As you look around, it might feel as if your colleagues are less receptive to the new initiatives you are trying to implement. Still, as an academic leader, your supervisor or the board you report to expects you to innovate in the offerings and operations of your organization.

Academic leadership during times of turbulence for higher education is no longer just about "being a good citizen," "keeping the seat warm," or "taking one for the team." No. There are expectations that our university leaders will differentiate their institutions, find cost savings or new sources of revenue, and come up with novel ways to engage external communities.

And yet, the way universities work means you cannot go it alone. You are encouraged to be collaborative, generating and refining ideas with your colleagues. You may be expected, or even required, to have an idea vetted and approved by multiple faculty or shared-governance committees. Jumping in without taking time to establish buy-in from key stakeholders might result in a loss of credibility that is difficult to recover from and often leads to change that doesn't stick.

But how are you supposed to surface and iterate on new ideas when it seems like there is always someone raising their hand to say, "So-and-so [insert name of influential faculty member or administrator] has concerns"? Sometimes it seems as though new ideas get shot down before they even get a chance to be considered.

It's not easy to face pushback and resistance. We have both experienced the deflated feeling that comes when a major change initiative we are excited about comes under enormous scrutiny and is picked apart. It can feel frustrating when what seemed like a modest suggestion is perceived or characterized as a much bigger transformation than we thought.

In these moments, we sometimes hear an internal voice telling us to just give up. *Why bother?* we ask ourselves. *No one appreciates the effort I've put into this anyway. Even if I improve the proposal in response to this feedback, they'll just find some other aspect to criticize.*

If you do hear some version of this negative thought pattern, take heed: it can be a red flag for leaders, pointing to a need to step back and reframe. Inevitably, some of your decisions will be unpopular with certain groups. In fact, when you face resistance from some units or individuals, you can generally take that as a sign your leadership decisions are truly effecting change. But do you need universal support? Almost certainly not.

It's worth taking time to consider what you require from each stakeholder in order for your initiatives or decisions to succeed. Do you need a group's active involvement? Vocal support? Or that the group just won't stand in the way?

And then there are those unforgettable times when the negative feedback reaches even deeper than an idea or initiative we're leading. What about reactions that seem aimed at our personality traits, leadership style, or how closely we adhere to stereotypes tied to a social identity—for example, when women and people of color in leadership roles receive feedback that their way of speaking or presenting ideas is seen by others as threatening or overly aggressive?

Well in the Lead

What about comments that cast doubt on our essential capabilities and suitability for a leadership role? This kind of negative feedback can shake us to the core. Whether it's delivered in whispers from a "concerned colleague," slipped into our inbox through a forwarded email chain, or hurled across the table during a performance conversation with a boss, it can undermine even a seasoned leader's effectiveness. It's not actionable. It's not constructive. It can cause us to rewind back to every conversation, every interaction, every meeting, and second-guess ourselves both in our past performance and into the future.

Leadership is not for the faint of heart

Both of us have experienced these dark moments. Though the memories still sting, we've also learned two important things that we think have made us better leaders. First, negative feedback says just as much about the giver's shortcomings as it does about the receiver's. Providing developmental feedback is a learned skill, and many managers simply aren't good at it.

Second, there may be a nugget of truth in what a boss or colleague has shared, even if it was delivered in a clumsy, insensitive, or downright nasty way. We've both tried to learn how to set aside the hurt or embarrassment that comes with hearing negative feedback and reflect on what we might be able to glean that is worth keeping. Perhaps there's nothing. But maybe there's a kernel that we can carry with us and that will help us improve. For example, could we get better at determining the measures of success for a new initiative before launching it? Could we improve our communication skills in certain types of settings or with particular audiences?

Here are some additional reframings that may help you see these situations differently:

- *You are not alone.* Every leader encounters pushback. In fact, we'll bet some of the very colleagues who are now criticizing your idea were once in a leadership role themselves and experienced this as well.
- *You've identified a problem to solve, and now you and your colleagues can work together*

toward a solution. Rather than shutting down, give yourself credit for having the courage to identify a concern and to seek to address it. How might you avoid growing embattled against your colleagues and instead side with your colleagues against the problem?
- *Timing matters.* The internal or external environment may not be conducive to this particular initiative right now, but that doesn't mean it can't be revisited at a later date. Try to discern whether the tides are running with or against certain ideas.
- *It's the stories you tell yourself that are the problem, not the fact that your proposed initiative receives some criticism.*
- *You don't need to react to every comment.* Some people have knee-jerk impulses to point out every little thing that they think is wrong with an idea. You get to choose whether to respond.

Remember the words of Teddy Roosevelt, amplified in Brené Brown's book *Daring Greatly*: you are one of those who have the courage to be "in the arena," you are working for something worthwhile, and even if the worst-case scenario should happen and you fail, you will have failed "while daring greatly."

For reflection

How can you remain enthusiastic and motivated in the face of significant resistance?

How might you maintain a focus on curiosity and growth, especially when the results of your efforts aren't what you'd hoped?

How can you identify those nuggets of truth in critical feedback without getting buried in self-doubt?

How might you begin to expand your ability to sit with the discomfort of others' unhappiness or negative judgments?

What would help you most in this moment?

Well in the Lead

In prayer

When feeling spent . . .

Dear God,

I have no idea why I took this job.
It has caused me nothing but misery.

I exhaust myself working 24/7,
trying to consider everyone's perspectives
and everyone's needs,
and am I rewarded with gratitude
or even the slightest acknowledgment
of my efforts?

Of course not.
Instead, I get constant pushback,
incessant complaints,
and potshots from all directions.

Help me see beyond this narrow view.
Help me move through
the painful sense of failure and rejection
to a place where I can access
the larger truth,
where I can see the positive impact of my work
and also learn from the resistance I'm facing.

Most of all,
help me remember that

Leadership is not for the faint of heart

no matter how hard things get,
I am never alone
and I am loved.

Amen.

Well in the Lead

When seeking to engage openly . . .

Dear God,

Logically, I know the value of remaining open,
of collaborating with others as equal partners
and actively seeking their feedback and input.

And yet,
a negative comment from a trusted colleague
can leave me feeling unsteady,
and the desire to self-protect
follows right behind.
I can feel myself armoring up,
closing myself off to those uncomfortable emotions
and no longer showing up fully as a result.

Please help me find the courage to remain present
no matter the circumstances.
Help me tap into my inner resources
and into others' strengths.
And help me live out
the brave brand of leadership
I wish to embody every day.

Amen.

When feeling grateful . . .

Dear God,

My heart skips with joy
and I feel so fortunate for the chance I've been given
to lead at such a critical place and time.

I feel confident.
I feel energized.
I feel optimistic.

At what we will accomplish. Together.

Amen.

Well in the Lead

9. You need to come up for air.

Feedback

Iron wind
strikes my back,
doubling me over.
Hunched,
I gasp,
then pause,
breathe,
unfold myself,
and listen.
(Elizabeth Odders-White)

❖❖❖

We've already established that leadership roles are not for the faint of heart. In fact, life as a leader can feel like a hurricane, as we're blown from one crisis to the next, the driving rain battering and bruising us. We've likely all questioned our strength to weather the storm.

To successfully lead, it is essential we remain well both emotionally and physically; thus, the title of this book. Stress, anxiety, and loneliness often come with the territory. Yet leadership roles require wisdom, perspective, and careful emotional regulation, all of which are difficult to access when we're completely tapped out. It's awfully hard to maintain our composure—let alone develop, effectively communicate, and execute a vision—when we're running on fumes.

For many of us, taking time to refuel is challenging. For some, it feels almost impossible. There's so much to be done, so many people counting on us; it's easy to consistently put ourselves at the bottom of the list. It may even feel selfish to make our own well-being a priority.

And yet, failing to do so can have disastrous consequences. Would you want to be operated on by a surgeon who hadn't slept in three days? Pushing yourself beyond your limits doesn't serve your organization. To the contrary, it reduces your effectiveness as a leader and sets a poor example for others. By failing to honor your own needs, you are also neglecting your commitment to your organization and your colleagues, who depend on you to be at your best.

But even when we believe firmly in the importance of caring for ourselves, it isn't always easy. We've both struggled to prioritize our own well-being while juggling the multitudinous demands of leadership roles. This often requires difficult choices and saying no when we'd rather say yes (a topic we've addressed in chapter 4).

What's more, as academics, we tend to live in our head. While thinking things through and systematically weighing options are important aspects of leadership, some of us go too far, getting stuck in overthinking and rumination. "Analysis paralysis" is often close behind. We might even lose touch with our body's messages regarding when we need to get a drink of water or take a quick walk. Taking steps to periodically stop intellectualizing can support not only our well-being but our leadership, by strengthening our ability to see the bigger picture.

Luckily, there are ways of coming up for air that don't require a lot of time or difficult trade-offs. For example, we've found that simply acknowledging what we're experiencing can be an important first step. It's natural to feel anxious, lonely, or overwhelmed when facing leadership challenges.

Remembering that these feelings are normal can reduce their sting.

Similarly, a quick conversation with someone who truly accepts and supports us can work wonders, whether that's a friend or family member, a colleague, or a coach. We both appreciate walking meetings with colleagues, getting a new perspective and enjoying time outdoors.

In light of vast differences in personalities and preferences, rather than suggesting more tips, we bring your attention to the questions for reflection on the following page. We hope they will help you identify ways to care for yourself that are both effective and easy to integrate into the unique circumstances of your life.

As we close this chapter, we want to share this simple reminder: your needs are important. Honoring them serves not only you, but your organization and others you care about. Aren't you all well worth the effort?

For reflection

What do you need to function at your best? Enough sleep? Occasional walks around the block? Healthy snacks? How can you ensure these needs are honored and fulfilled? What might you have to let go of to do so?

What energizes you or lifts your spirits? How can you incorporate more of that into your daily routine? Conversely, what might you need less of?

What is not serving you right now? How can you tell? At times when you feel depleted, what patterns do you notice? What is a tiny change you might make to disrupt that pattern?

How can coming up for air be easy?

What boundaries have you set regarding work and time off? Have you shared those boundaries with others? What support do you need to uphold them?

How would you spend your dream vacation? How can you bring at least parts of that dream to fruition?

How might you benefit from taking occasional breaks, stepping away from your work for a few minutes?

Well in the Lead

What would you do with five free minutes right now? What about thirty minutes? An hour?

What would it look like to offer yourself kindness and compassion in this moment?

What will help you honor your commitment to self-care?

In prayer

When feeling lost . . .

Dear God,

I am completely overwhelmed.

I had no idea everything could feel this complicated,
that it could take what seems an eternity
to put out a single fire,
only to learn that ten more
have popped up in the meantime.

How can I possibly focus on strategic issues,
or even just the hundreds of other things on my plate,
when my head is spinning?

I can't continue like this.

Please help me see through the chaos.
Show me where I need to direct my attention,
where my unique talents and experience
are most needed.

And help me remember
that I must care for myself to care for others,
that taking a break is not selfish but wise,
and that the example I set has a lasting impact.

Well in the Lead

Please be my guide
as I seek to uplift and celebrate wellness
rather than prioritizing hardship.

Amen.

When feeling grounded . . .

Dear God,

When I finally stop running—
when I shut down the computer,
silence the phone,
close the door,
and just sit and breathe—
peace washes over me.

I am overwhelmed,
but not by work and to-do lists.
Instead, I am overcome
by gratitude and love
for the life I have
and the people in it.

When I consider all the gifts I've been given,
especially the chance to do meaningful work
with creative, engaged colleagues,
I feel a deep sense of connection
to everyone and everything around me.

I feel larger than the sky.

May I continue
to create space for this experience of expansiveness,
that it may ground me when things get blustery.

And may I help to cultivate
this calm knowing in others,
so they too may experience
the immense rewards it brings.

Amen.

Well in the Lead

10. Things get easier with experience.

The recipe

Forty-two epiphanies,
each repeated sixteen times,
yields a heaping plate of pluck.
(Elizabeth Odders-White)

♦♦♦

The title of this chapter states the obvious. It's surprising how valuable stating the obvious can be. In fact, that might be one of the few actual pieces of leadership advice we give in this book: state the obvious from time to time, both to yourself and to others. As humans, we forget easily; and importantly, we often talk ourselves out of knowing what we know. So we can all benefit from a reminder now and then.

That things get easier with time naturally implies things are harder early on. And why wouldn't they be? When we first assume a leadership role, so much is new. We're making it up as we go along. Expecting someone to know how to do something they've never done, often with little instruction or guidance, defies logic; yet that's the standard many of us set for ourselves. And the academic culture perpetuates it by putting faculty members into leadership roles without assessing their skills or providing the support needed to learn while in the role.

Staff leaders, though often expected to demonstrate significant administrative experience before being selected for a leadership position, may be "set up to fail" in an organizational culture where the faculty-staff hierarchy often supersedes positional authority. The attitude appears to be "They're smart people; they'll figure it out." Implicit in that could also be a belief that so-called soft skills—a huge mislabeling, if you ask us—aren't that important and are something you either just have or you don't.

Even for those with leadership training, substantial on-the-job learning is required. Many savvy leaders eventually discover, to their surprise and possible dismay, that the very qualities that were seen by supervisors and colleagues as strengths can become liabilities in a leadership context.

Things get easier with experience

For example, a strong sense of curiosity that shows up as a tendency to ask many probing questions can make someone a great contributor to a team. But a leader who overuses their sense of curiosity runs the risk of confusing and frustrating those around them, including the direct reports who may feel unintended pressure to find answers and the ever-busier senior campus leaders for whom the questions create an unhelpful distraction. With experience, a naturally curious leader can learn to be more selective about which questions to voice, and more skillful at phrasing them.

As we run more meetings, participate in more strategic discussions, and make more tough decisions, our comfort and confidence increase. We gain in awareness of both our superpower and our Achilles' heel, and of how they are sometimes two sides of the same coin. Certain activities may even become second nature. Still, no one with higher-education leadership experience would describe the job itself as easy. So how do we navigate those times when we're faced with leadership challenges we haven't encountered before and feel entirely unprepared for?

First, let's treat ourselves fairly. Do we expect students to have mastered the material before the first class? Then we ought not apply a different standard to ourselves.

Second, let's celebrate our progress. The plus side of stepping into something new is constant learning. We need to occasionally seize a moment to take stock of how far we've come.

And finally, let's remember that while the job will never become easy, we will acquire a greater sense of ease. Though the learning curve may be steep, we will eventually scale the mountain with skill. And when we do, we can collapse at the top and take a well-deserved two-week nap.

For reflection

How can you remind yourself that things do get easier with experience?

How would things change if you could trust that you are exactly where you need to be on the learning curve?

What comes easily to you that others may struggle with? Which of these strengths make you stand out as a leader?

How can you track and celebrate your progress?

How would it feel to treat yourself with kindness and compassion whatever the circumstances?

Well in the Lead

In prayer

Dear God,

Sometimes I struggle to see
all that I've accomplished,
the progress I've made,
the growth I've experienced.
It's so easy to get caught up
in the day-to-day whirlwind
of activity and demands
without ever slowing down
to reflect or take stock.

Please help me pause.
Help me acknowledge and celebrate
how far I've come.
Help me savor those feelings
of success and achievement,
and draw upon them
when things feel hard.

Help me see the true impact of my work
in its full scope and depth,
from the tiniest shift
to the most significant change in someone's life.

And help me view all of this
with kindness, gratitude, and humility.

Amen.

Epilogue

"What is Real?" asked the Rabbit...

"Real isn't how you are made," said the Skin Horse. "It's a thing that happens to you. When a child loves you for a long, long time, not just to play with, but *really* loves you, then you become Real."

"Does it hurt?" asked the Rabbit.

"Sometimes," said the Skin Horse, for he was always truthful. "When you are Real you don't mind being hurt."

"Does it happen all at once, like being wound up," he asked, "or bit by bit?"

"It doesn't happen all at once," said the Skin Horse. "You become. It takes a long time. That's why it doesn't often happen to people who break easily, or have sharp edges, or who have to be carefully kept. Generally, by the time you are Real, most of your hair has been loved off, and your eyes drop out and you get loose in the joints and very shabby. But these things don't matter at all, because once you are Real you can't be ugly, except to people who don't understand... Once you are Real you can't become unreal again. It lasts for always."

(*The Velveteen Rabbit*, Williams 1925, 3–4)

Well in the Lead

Notes

Please be aware that the websites listed below may have changed since the date of publication.

Chapter 1

But beware of the dark side . . .
This sage advice from Yoda appears in *Star Wars: Episode V—The Empire Strikes Back*, directed by Irvin Kershner (1980; San Francisco and Los Angeles, CA: Lucasfilm and 20th Century Fox Home Entertainment, 2006), DVD.

Chapter 3

The point is not to become a leader . . .
Warren Bennis offers these wise words on page 106 of *On Becoming a Leader: The Leadership Classic*, rev. ed. (New York: Basic Books, 2009).

Origami spirits . . .
This haiku by Elizabeth Odders-White was originally published on page 49 of *Wisconsin People & Ideas: The Magazine of the Wisconsin Academy of Sciences, Arts and Letters* 66, no. 2 (Spring 2020). It also appears on page 2 of Elizabeth's book *Well on Your Way: An Assistant Professor's Companion* (Madison, WI: nodramaturg, 2020).

Well in the Lead

Tasha Eurich describes . . .
For a summary of this work, see Tasha Eurich, "What Self-Awareness Really Is (and How to Cultivate It)," *Harvard Business Review*, January 4, 2018, https://hbr.org/2018/01/what-self-awareness-really-is-and-how-to-cultivate-it.

Chapter 6

Both approaches remind us . . .
Oprah has spoken frequently about the sage advice she received from Maya Angelou. See, for example, https://www.oprah.com/oprahs-lifeclass/when-people-show-you-who-they-are-believe-them-video.

Calling on our "wise mind" . . .
Wise mind is a concept from dialectical behavior therapy, an approach developed by Dr. Marsha Linehan. Wise mind bridges "emotion mind," which relies entirely on feelings, and "reasonable mind," driven solely by logic. Read more in Marsha M. Linehan's *DBT Skills Training Handouts and Worksheets*, 2nd ed. (New York: Guilford Press, 2015), 50–52.

Chapter 7

Our thanks to adrienne maree brown . . .
"Less prep, more presence" is one of the core principles of adrienne maree brown's *Emergent*

Strategy: Shaping Change, Changing Worlds (Chico, CA: AK Press, 2017), 42.

Chapter 8

Remember the words of Teddy Roosevelt . . .

In her preface to *Daring Greatly: How the Courage to Be Vulnerable Transforms the Way We Live, Love, Parent, and Lead* (New York: Gotham Books, 2012), Brené Brown utilizes Teddy Roosevelt's "the man who is actually in the arena," from his 1910 speech "Citizenship in a Republic," to frame and motivate her examination of the importance of vulnerability and its connection to courage.

Epilogue

Thanks to the copyright law of public domain, we are able to provide this meaningful excerpt from Margery Williams's US publication of *The Velveteen Rabbit or How Toys Become Real* (New York: George H. Doran, 1925), 3–4.

Photographs

Photographs were taken by Elizabeth Odders-White unless otherwise indicated.

Cover

Follow/Lead (Tudor Place Garden, Washington, DC): photograph by Suzanne Dove

Chapter 1

Hot Seat (Madison, WI)
Let There Be Light (Madison, WI)
Treasured Reflections (Madison, WI)

Chapter 2

A Perfect Fit (Madison, WI)
Defenses (Madison, WI)
Wobble (Madison, WI)

Chapter 3

Swirling (Olbrich Botanical Gardens, Madison, WI)
Emerging (Denver Botanic Gardens, Denver, CO)
Onward (Olbrich Botanical Gardens, Madison, WI)

Chapter 4

Stacks (Madison Youth Arts Center, Madison, WI)
Boundaries (Madison, WI)
Yield (Verona, WI)

Photographs

Chapter 5

Unending (Educational Institute Oholei Torah, Crown Heights, Brooklyn, NY)
Perfection (Madison, WI)
Shine (Madison, WI)

Chapter 6

Lonely at the Top (Madison, WI)
Side by Side (Madison, WI)
Grown Together (Madison, WI)

Chapter 7

Coherence (Madison, WI)
Perspective (Madison, WI)
Forest (f)or the Trees? (Park City, UT)

Chapter 8

Broken (Madison, WI): photograph by Suzanne Dove
All the Feels (drawings by Ethan White, age four, 2001, Madison, WI)
Majesty (Arbroath Abbey, Arbroath, Scotland)

Chapter 9

Air (Phoenix, AZ)
Counterpoint (Madison, WI): photograph by Suzanne Dove

Chapter 10

Span (Pittsburgh, PA): photograph by Suzanne Dove
Amass (Madison Youth Arts Center, Madison, WI)
Ease (Madison, WI)

Acknowledgments

We would like to thank the many courageous and committed higher education leaders we are honored to have as colleagues, mentors, clients, and friends. Your work may happen behind the scenes, and you may rarely receive the thanks you deserve. We see you, and we appreciate what an incredibly important role you play for your institution. Without the opportunities to learn from and with you, this book would never have existed.

We extend special thanks to our early readers: Ron Cramer, Diane Del Guercio, Katherine Lampley, EllenMarie McPhillip, Inara Scott, and Meredith Temple.

Because even the most well-chosen words feel insufficient to express our gratitude to all who have helped and supported us along the way, we end with a brief and lighthearted note of appreciation:

> Oh, how can we ever express
> Our sincere and profound thankfulness?
> To our families and friends,
> Whose compassion transcends,
> You're the key to our every success!

About the authors

After a twenty-year career as a researcher, teacher, and leader at the University of Wisconsin–Madison, **Elizabeth Odders-White** founded *nodramaturg coaching & consulting* to help clients in higher education—and beyond—thrive. She finds great fulfillment in assisting inspired-but-overwhelmed faculty and leaders to build self-trust and confidence for the impact (and life!) they desire. She is motivated by a not-so-secret dream of shifting the academic culture one person at a time.

Elizabeth earned a PhD in finance from Northwestern University, as well as a BS in mathematics and a BFA in music, both from Tulane University. She is a Professional Certified Coach, credentialed through the International Coaching Federation, and a Certified Executive Coach with additional training in positive-psychology coaching.

Elizabeth is the mother of two wise and witty young-adult children and lives in Madison, Wisconsin, with her husband, Matt, who routinely sees her at her worst and miraculously likes her anyway.

You can learn more about Elizabeth and her work at elizabethodderswhite.com.

About the authors

Suzanne Dove is the founding executive director of the Badavas Center for Innovation in Teaching and Learning at Bentley University. A common thread throughout her career has been her work with executive leaders and teams to foster a culture of innovation and organizational change. Suzanne's university experience spans teaching, research, outreach, and management roles. She is a higher education strategist and innovator, leading enterprise-level endeavors in program and curriculum design, learning-technology initiatives, and faculty development. A constant is her passion for addressing systemic barriers in order to create the conditions where all learners can realize their potential.

Suzanne earned a PhD in political and administration sciences from the Universitat Autònoma de Barcelona. She holds a Master of Public Administration from New York University and a BA from Brandeis University.

Suzanne is based in Madison, Wisconsin, where she and her talented husband, Miguel, enjoy being parents to two active, inquisitive teenagers and a rescue dog named Patxi.

Also by Elizabeth Odders-White . . .

Well on Your Way
an assistant professor's companion

Have you ever felt lost or alone as you navigate the winding and thorny path toward tenure? Then *Well on Your Way* is the traveling companion you've been missing. Every inch is infused with the encouragement and wisdom you'd expect from a lifelong friend. Keep it close by, and discover how small shifts can make your work and life easier, happier, and more fulfilling.

"After twenty years in academia, I finally found the book I wish I'd read when I first became an assistant professor."
— Kristen Slack, Founder of Prof2Prof, Professor, Sandra Rosenbaum School of Social Work, University of Wisconsin–Madison

nodramaturg publishing